TRADING EXPERTS PRESENTS

GAME PLANNING

LEARN 3 SECRETS TO FORM A PROPER GAME PLAN

STEP 4

Trading Experts Presents:

Game Planning

Even if you aren't a sports fan, the concept of having a game plan before heading into a game should not be a foreign concept to you. We can all agree that if a team or individual does not have a game plan the likelihood of success is minimal or luck at best. Even in less competitive areas they will be more likely to succeed with a quick plan of action. There was a wise old man who once said *"If you don't plan, you are planning to fail"* that old man by the way, was Ben Franklin.

That is why before buying your first stock, you always need a gameplan, and not just for when you are right, but more importantly for when you are wrong, this is when having a gameplan keeps you in the game.

We put together our most critical lessons that new investors need to learn before putting their money into the markets. You must fully understand the concept of risk management, execution, game planning, risk-reward and proper chart reading before you even think about investing your hard earned money.

Find below a table of contents along with each lesson including questions for you to answer to solidify your learning of these concepts. These lessons will take you through the learning process of a new trader on Wall Street and everything they're taught in their first year. How do we know? We've been through the gauntlet. We want you to learn from all the mistakes we've made and profit in the process.

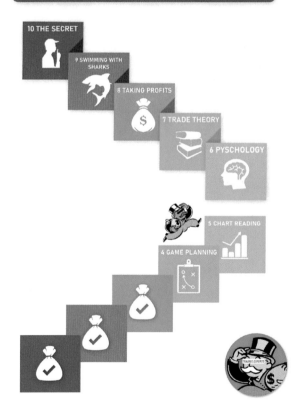

You don't need to be a math whiz or have a perfect GPA to be a successful trader. You do need proper game planning and the right guidance along the way.

From Bennett Zamani & Shake Pryzby

Table of Contents

Step 4 Game Planning Video Lessons

Before we jump into the lessons in Step 4, it could be a good idea to spend a few minutes watching some of the video lessons that go along with this book to help you better understand the ideas you are about to read about!

1. Search Trading Experts on YouTube
2. Hit playlists on our page
3. Select Step 4 Game Planning Playlist
4. Watch, Learn, Subscribe and Drop a Thumbs Up!

What's a Gameplan?

The best way to guard against overconfidence when making investment decisions is to have a plan ahead of time. Know when you're wrong; using price levels, dollar loss levels or percentage loss levels are essential if not imperative if you plan to successfully navigate the rocky and choppy waters of the market as a swing trader or investor. Making decisions ahead of time, especially decisions that involve admitting defeat, can help conquer one of the biggest hurdles investors face; looking in the mirror and seeing an ability that we just do not possess.

One of the most important things as a trader that you need to have locked down is a simple game plan prior to putting on the idea. This is the most crucial aspect of a traders success that most traders never heard of or spend the time on long after the negative emotional side effects have kicked in.

Skipping the gameplan for most is easy and there is a good chance you have done this somewhere in your life (we all have), you hear about some new stock that a friend or family member said was going to go up. You hear this tip and drop $5,000 without skipping a beat, yet you will have endless debate in your head if you should spend $1.75 for a side of guacamole at Chipotle. Now you have $5,000 in the company you know nothing about, other than it has to go up, but somewhere crazy happening, it just goes down, and down and down. Your friend all of a sudden isn't as excited about that old company anymore and is much slower to answer texts or calls as he has been and continues to dig a financial hole he can't fill as you join him in the quicksand he roped you into.

As corny as those quotes such as *failing to plan is planning to fail,* when it comes to trading, it should be tattooed on our foreheads. What we are about to teach you about forming a proper gameplan will be by far one of the most important tools you will take with you on your investing journey in the future.

A simple gameplan has 3 components:

1. Entry Price
2. Stop Price (if/when wrong)
3. Target Price

It could be a day trade, swing trade, long term trade, my grandmother told me to buy it, pretend insider information trade, it's going to a million trade. We don't care what the trade is or the time you think you will hold it for. You need to know at what price you will, at what price you will take the loss if wrong and ideally when you will sell for profit.

Now your gameplan can be more detailed and included more than those three, but for now let's keep it simple when it comes to planning. Any stock you ever mention in our groups going forward, you will be expected to include those 3 key components, if you do not, it shows us that you lack the effort in your own planning and that we will not assist you with.

Game Planning Task

What are the 3 components to any trading idea?

1.

2.

3.

To Buy or Not To Buy

The Entry

Your entry is by far the most important factor when buying a stock, you can buy the best stock in the world however if you just bought the all time high you're not going to make money. On the flip side you could buy the worst stock in the market, but if you get the best price it could be a home run. For now let's focus on the former because you're not looking to buy the best piece of crap out there, you're looking to buy the best company trading at the best price.

Below are two examples, CAT and GE. Be honest, would you rather buy CAT at $115 that is up over 100% in the last year or GE that seems like a deal that's down around 25% in the same time?

CAT up over 100% at a major level

Tradingexperts24 published on TradingView.com, November 13, 2019 23:02:00 UTC
BATS:CAT, 1W 144.49 ▼ −1.85 (−1.26%) O:146.74 H:148.47 L:143.69 C:144.49

Or

GE on sale off 25% from recent highs

Now before we show you which was the correct answer, let's take a step back. If you are new to trading and have never bought a stock before then most of you will tend to shop for stocks as you do when shopping for clothes. You see a jacket that you like and see the price tag for $500, most know that in time stores have to get rid of their merchandise and if patient enough that jacket will eventually be on sale. You come back a week later and it's 10% off, no dice, two weeks later 20% off, still holding out, a month later 35% off, ok that's fair however you can still wait, then it's the end of winter and the jacket is 50%, what a steal! You grab it, yet it's 70 degrees and that goose down parka is as useless as having condoms on a deserted island.

On the flip side I want you to take a minute and think of your most expensive purchase, maybe it was your home or a high end watch. Now this major purchase you tend to hold for some time and what does it typically do? It usually holds its value or sometimes even appreciates.

This is the type of shopping you want to do when shopping for stocks. Just like that shirt that you got a deal on, a month later it is worthless. You spent $50 on it and could not sell it for more than $10 if your life depended on it. Yet that $500,000 home has value, that $30,000 Rolex made of solid gold has value, or even if you have plunked down $20,000 to get your girlfriend or wife a Hermes Birkin bag, that also has perceived value and more importantly demand (Birkin bags have appreciated on average 10% a year for the last 30 years). Now let's see how your shopping for stocks panned out.

If you selected CAT you were correct - it increased by over 50%

If you bought what seemed to be expensive, it increased by another 50% in less than a year, just as most expensive items tend to do. What's expensive tends to get more expensive until it doesn't. Now on the flip side the stock on sale is even more on sale.

If you selected GE you would have lost over 75% in the same period

GE was a deal a year ago, down 25% (and most would think that was the deal) yet it went on sale even more and fell another 75% from that entry. What's cheap tends to get even cheaper until it doesn't.

Most who are new to the markets are traders on the way up and investors on the way down. Do the opposite.

This is why we focus on buying stocks that are near major levels of resistance on their weekly charts, yes weekly charts, not the last 5 min bar that closed. Focus on the big picture first, weekly levels, then look closer at the daily level to find your entry first. Most new traders do the complete opposite, they shop for losers then look at the smallest time frame possible for an entry. Focus on charts in the top right near highs, keep it simple. Now we can't just blindly buy highs and be right. That's why we always have a stop for when we are wrong.

Game Planning Task

Post a Dow 30 stock that recently broke out of a major resistance level to new highs (cheat code: look at the most expensive stocks) with the caption *winner.*

Then post a stock that recently broke down below a major level to hit a new low (cheat code: look at some cheap stocks) with the caption *loser.*

Post your answer in the chat

Bull Flags

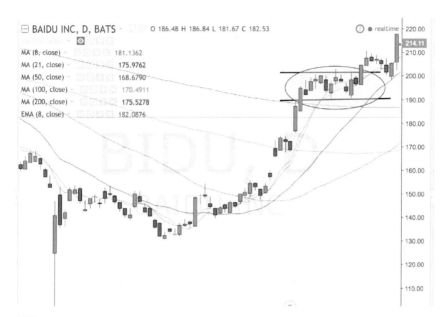

Bull Flags are our bread and butter and a staple in any trader's tool belt. Most new traders want to reinvent the wheel and trade patterns they have yet to understand. For now your primary focus is to master this set up.

The **bull flag** is a continuation pattern which only slightly retraces the advance preceding it. The technical buy point is when price penetrates the upper trend line of the **flag** area, ideally on volume expansion. Context: Found within an uptrend. So as we can see here $200 is an area this stock had trouble breaking on the way up. Once it consolidates a bit, by moving sideways, it finally breaks higher on noticeably expanded volume. That's when we want to be in the trade, with our stop at the low of the day on the day it breaks.

Why the low of the day on the day it breaks? This is a bullish chart pattern, if the stock just broke out of a flag but ends the days at lows, that's a really bad sign and the trade is going to fail most of the time if it does that. This flag has a $10 range before it broke, so most traders buying this pattern would look to sell $10 higher from the break.

Game Planning Task

1. **Post 2 stocks that are currently forming bull flags with your complete game plan (Entry, Stop, Target, Risk Reward).**

   (Pro Tip: the longer the consolidation the better.)

2. **If the flag is forming a $10 range like BIDU above, how much higher do you expect the break to go in the short term?**

3. **If you buy a stock when it breaks out of a bull flag, but ended the day at lows what should you do?**

4. **If the stock breaks out of a bull flag and ends the days at highs what should you do?**

Post your answer in the chat

Penthouse or Poor House

Pick your favorite stock that you would buy at today's price.

What would your stop loss be?

At what price would you want to sell it for a profit?

Now based on your risk vs reward, what is the ratio? 1:1, 2:1, 10:1, etc., write it down so you can compare yourself to what professional traders and billionaires aim for when looking at risk reward.

By having a **stop** (which is at a price below your entry) you will sell for a small loss and limit further losses if the stock continues to fall.

By setting a stop loss you are determining your risk in that particular trade to limit your downside. By defining your max loss you are willing to take on your investment, you can now figure out the ideal profit!

"The average person goes out and invests a dollar hoping to make 10% or 20%, if they're lucky — so if they're wrong they're in the hole majorly"

You want to focus on taking trades where you can make **5:1** on your risk or better. But why? Keep reading and you will find out.

Let's say you are risking $100 in a trade, what should be your minimum profit target?

A. $100
B. $500
C. $550
D. $750

If you can strive to aim for 5:1 risk reward (answer B) or greater you will have a better chance at being successful. Why do we say this? Well let's hear from Paul Tudor Jones, one of the most successful hedge fund managers of the last century.

Paul Tudor Jones had a principle he followed which was called 5:1, and 5:1 is this:

"If I invest a dollar, I won't part with that dollar I'm investing unless I feel certain I'm going to make five."

He knows — he's not stupid — he knows he's going to be wrong [sometimes] so if he loses a dollar and has to spend another dollar, spending two to make five, he's still up $3.

He can be wrong four out of five times and still be in great shape. Almost everybody thinks that if you want to get big rewards you need to take huge risks. But if you keep thinking that, you're going to be broke.

Game Planning Task

Now let's fill out a new game plan of your favorite stock below with your new knowledge on risk reward and compare the difference between not knowing about proper risk reward vs now with your new found knowledge of it.

- Game Plan
- What is your entry price?
- What is your stop?
- What is your ideal target price to sell at?
- What is the risk reward ratio?

Post your answer in the chat

Risk Elastic

When you think of outsized returns (70, 80, 100, 200, 1,000%) what comes to mind? Huge amounts of risk to achieve those types of returns? Most would think high risk high reward, low risk low reward. Right? For most cases that is usually true. Jumping out of an airplane, huge risk, also a ton of fun. Go to the movies alone, low risk, low reward. However with enough swings of your bat (trades) and enough patience finding your meat ball pitch, you can have your cake and eat it too by having low risk and extremely high reward.

Percentage Gain Leader Board

Leader - Carl Theodore **2044%** MRNA in $13 out $284, 600 days
2nd - Mahmoud Hemood **1406%** TSLA in $66 out $994, 701 days
3nd - Garret Stein **1020%** MGNI in $6 out $61, 274 days
4th - Gina Theodore **739%** DWAC in $16 out $139 2 days
5th - Reid D **588%** MARA in $5 out $36 40 days
6th - Jake Fox **404%** FLGT in $36 out $184 91 days
7th - Ivan Martin **400%** TWLO in $26 out $130, 365 days
8th - Tyler Kinney **376%** CELH in $21 out $99, 349 days
9th - Cam Edmondson **372%** JD in $19 out $92, 716 days
10th - Reid D **276%** BLNK in $10 out $38, 6 days

Now realize these trades don't come around every day and require patience. A company doesn't just double overnight, and you are not going to know which trades are going to be grand slams, that is why you need to be in the game. The lazy trader tends to ask, what's the next big one, and our answer is when we sell it you'll be the first to know. We can't predict the future, we can plan for it, sure. However you, I, some market wizards have no clue which names will consistently be the best of the year and the guy who says that he does tends to be full of you know what.

What is risk elastic? Risk elastic is where you can find a setup that has such a major level that it is bound to pop. Think of pushing a slinky together as tight as you can, when you release it, it expands. Now it's not an earth shattering expansion, however an expansion nonetheless. Below are a few trades that were extremely low risk to high reward, these are the 50-1 risk reward trades that come around a handful of times a year that you don't know about until after the fact.

NKTR was a Big Picture idea, the entry was $25, the stop was $24. Doesn't take a genius to know that's $1 risk. 60 days later it's at $75, Ben G's idea was that it would take a year to become a $50 stock. He was so wrong it went up 200% in 2 months instead of the planned 100% in a year. It sucks to suck, right? Would you risk 1% to make 200%?

ANAB was one of Shake's calls in his weekly Shake Down newsletter that he sends out every weekend. His entry was $68, he was risking $4 per share and sold it at $115 just 2 months later for a 70% gain. He was risking less than 5% to make 70% and he patiently waited 2 months to catch the meat of this move.

"Just like getting fit, virtually anyone can do it if they are willing to do what it takes."

Ray Dalio

CAT was another major trade that took almost a year. Buying up through the major breakout level where most would have said it was too expensive and too extended, to going on a 5 month run that went farther than the last 2 years that it had traded. We were risking 5% to make 50% in less than a year and still sold too early. However it tends to be easier to lighten the load on the way up than try and force an exit on the way down with the crowd. Hopefully you are getting the point. With all of these winners, there was a recurring theme.

1. Defined Entry

2. Immediately Right

3. Limited Risk (no more than 5%)

4. Patience

Game Planning Task

Post 3 charts where the stock broke out of a major level and went on a major run. (Pro Tip: When you have a big winner, trail it by the prior weekly candle low and see if you would still be in if you bought the major breakout.)

Post your answer in the chat

You are already 20% towards reaching your goal of finishing these lessons, keep it up! If you're proud of this say "I'm at the 20% mark!" in the Game Planning Group Chat!

Shoulda, Coulda, Woulda, Sell Stop

The four most expensive words in the English language are "this time it's different"

John Templeton

Now if trading was as simple as just buying new highs and holding we would all be billionaires relaxing on yachts sipping champagne. Trading can be simple if you have a consistent strategy and a game plan that you actually execute on. That's how simple trading can be, however much easier said than done. Even as a professional trader, we are professionally wrong, meaning we are actually wrong more times than we are right.

If you have a hard time swallowing that humble pie, the market will force that big spoon down your throat until you choke. This is why we use stops in every trade, we don't care if xyz stock is going to cure that disease or turn your trash into gold, we still use a stop. If we're right and the stock rips, the stop does not really matter, if you're wrong, you will be happy you had it.

We use stops in every trade because we know that one day we are going to be wrong and the stop removes the emotional aspect to a failing trade.

published on TradingView.com, January 20, 2018 16:57 UTC
BATS:VERI D 24.01 +0.35 (+2.04%) O:23.48 H:24.56 L:23.13 C:24.01

Say you got long VERI through $50 (one of our members did) and it looks sick, just ripping higher day after day. All good signs except for the fact this member did not have a stop in!

Ben G *"What's your stop?"*

Florin *"Stop? Thing's going to $100 yahoooooo!"*

(he actually said this)

After a few expletives that I will spare you here, we told him he had had to put a stop in, however the young brash trader had to learn this lesson the hard way, no matter how many times we tell him "don't touch the hot stove".

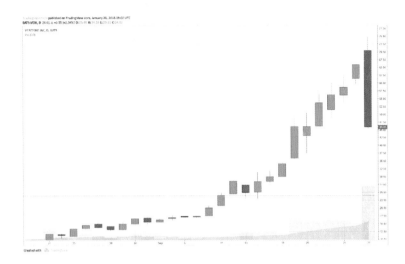

Doesn't look like it's going to $100 anymore now does it? Now during the conversation, the stock was flagging at $72 in the tightest flag known to man on a stock that just increased by 1000% in less than a month. Now seeing this tight flag, we could not have spelled it out more clearly to put a stop below the figure. If the stock wants to keep raging in a straight line up he would still be in, however when the tide turns, he would be out before he could make an emotionally bad decision. Let's take a closer look.

Mind you this is a 15 minute chart, not a daily or a weekly, in 30 minutes this thing dropped 36%. We told him to put his stop at $71.89, however the cocky member flying high on his huge winner, could do no wrong. Until Mr Market took him for a ride.

He had no plan for when he was wrong and froze up as most new traders do as a stock is dropping like a rock. He eventually capitulated and puked near the bottom. After this trade in question, we removed Florin from our Alpha chat because we have no time for that cowboy stuff. We have been running the Alpha chat for years and have had zero members blow up under our watch and Florin did not deserve to affect our group with his cowboy antics.

The more intense the craze, the higher the type of intellect that succumbs to it

Benjamin Anderson

This stock as most stocks who trade in this similar fashion can rarely sustain this type of move, just like Bitcoin to $19,000. At the peak, people were saying they would eat their own body parts if it didn't go to $100,000, now that it has since crashed by over 50% in a month, those claims are no longer said other than from a whisper.

Braggarts tell you of their great success (luck) yet they are the most quiet on the way down

This is why we use stops, because as a trader you are your own worst enemy. That's the cold, hard truth, you are the one clicking the buttons either making or losing yourself money. This one trade for Florin was a huge winner then turned into a loser (horrible trading) and had he not puked it could have been a trade that cost him 50% of his bankroll (horrible risk management). This is why we aim to risk around 1-3% in each of our ideas, and we aim to make 5-15%+ in our winners. We can still have 20, 30, 40, 50, 60, 70, even 100%+ winners with the same risk. Which we went over in detail in the *Risk Elastic* lesson.

Now there are some downsides to using a Stop that you will see first hand. There will be times when you get *shaken out*, meaning your stop was too tight and the stock rips in your face and you will be cursing at yourself saying *"why did I keep it so tight?!"* It's all part of the game because for every one of those shake outs, there are a dozen other failed trades that you forget that you lost 1% in, that died over the next few months and could have cost you an arm and a leg.

Game Planning Task

Post 2 chart's where using a stop below the prior day's low would have helped you avoid a massive loss!

Post your answer in the chat

Trailing Stops

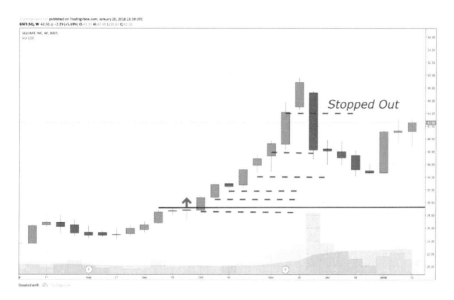

After you get into a winner and want to start to trail your winner, we at first move our stop up to break even, then we can trail by the weekly or daily low. Start to focus on the daily low and as you start to have real winners, the weekly lows will help drown out some of the noise.

In this trade through $29, we were aiming to make $5 risking $1, yet SQ didn't care and went much farther than any of us in the Alpha chat could have imagined. It ended up increasing by over $19 a share. That's a 65% gain on 3% risk.

For the members who trailed their winner by using the weekly low, were able to stay in through $48 and get stopped out down through $44 for around a 50% gain. When you trail your winner, you are not looking to catch the top, a trailing stop will keep you in through the top and eventually you will get stopped out lower. However if you trail properly you can catch the meat of the move while removing a lot of the emotional factors that tend to come with holding a big winner.

The main takeaways are:

- We have an idea of where a stock can go, but who says it can't go higher? By trailing we can have a game plan to stay in the position for greater profit while also managing our risk.
- Nothing is worse than having a profitable trade lose money due to the lack of proper stops.
- There can be times when a stock can shake you out, tick that prior low and then be right back up. It sucks when this happens but no trade is perfect.

Game Planning Task

After you are in a profitable position and how should you trail your position?

Why do we trail our profitable positions?

What is the downfall to a tight trailing stop?

Post your answer in the chat

The Art of the Trail

Y ou can map out the best trades in the best sectors with the best stocks, but at the end of the day it all comes down to your executions. Part of maintaining a winning trade is finding the proper **trail** that keeps you involved long enough to be a part of the momentum move, while not giving too much money back on pullbacks.

We mapped out how we would trailed our AMZN position on the 8 ema, because that's what the chart told us was holding. You can see, since it ignited (bottom arrow), how the 8 ema on the chart has supported this rise every time a candle came close to the moving average. It jumped off today's huge gap up, pulled in, and found support right at the moving average. We were not shocked. Learning the proper trail is KEY in trading, and one of the many lessons we teach here.

Now the obvious pitfall to trailing is what? Not capitalizing on selling at the stock's highest price. But we will tell you from first hand experience, in the last 1,000 trades, maybe .001% we sold at the actual ALL TIME HIGH. We can even give you the example below.

SWKS (Skyworks Solutions Inc)
Mar 31 2016 12:11:36
© FreeStockCharts.com
Price History

This is the one case, where we actually got stopped out at highs. With our swing trades, our stop is usually either the low of day or the prior low of day. After we got in at $84, by using that stop strategy we were able to stay in a profitable swing trade for over 23 days!

But trading is never this easy. Sure this one time we were able to sell $23 higher with $1 risk and sell at highs. The perfect, perfect storm of a profitable trade. But trading is rarely this easy, we are not here to buy the bottoms and sell the tops. We want to get into tight risk trades and be in for the meat of the move. Two days after we got out, this stock dropped $15 points, you don't want to sit through that pain. We took out profit and moved on. With the right trail, you will be in for the meat of the move, at some point see the high being put in (won't know it's the high until after you get stopped out) and then you will get stopped out for a profit. When you learn how to trail properly, you can control your greed since your plan is concrete. Once you can master the idea of the trail, you can master the markets.

The key takeaways we focus on with trailing a profitable position, are to look at the prior days low, as you look at AMZN, SWKS, and in the next lesson with OKS, each day it made a new higher low, confirming the stock was still on an uptrend. Stocks can be dirty and try to tail through the prior day's low to get the weak money out before continuing higher. When we have a cushion in a position or have been in a profitable swing for 3+ days, we will look to put our stop below the priors day low instead of the current days low.

You can see here, based on the day circled, we moved our stop up from $97 up to $100, and got stopped out the next day. We locked in a $16 gain on the remaining shares, and had confirmation the trend was now changing. Did we leave some profits on the table by not selling at $102.50? Of course, except when we got in our target to profit was only a messily $89, we as humans have a difficult time looking far into the future. By using a proper trailing technique, we can really maximize our winners.

I would like for you to go back to those ludicrous stocks you selected in the prior lesson and draw a line showing where you would have gotten stopped out if you were long for those run ups or short for those breakdowns, based off a stop at prior days low before it put in it's highs.

Game Planning Task

In the Game Planning Group chat post an example where trailing vs the prior day's low would have gotten you out right before the stock reversed a major breakout.

Post your answer in the chat

Mona Lisa Trailing Stop

O 43.67 H 44.05 L 42.86 C 43.01

When you look at this daily chart of OKS, can you see any area of resistance?

An area that the stock is having a hard time breaking? This is usually the result of a seller or sellers who are offering more stock to sell at that price than buyers can afford to buy.

The answer is the $42.50 area. Think of resistance as Warren Buffett, he's not in OKS but just for this example's stake. We're the little guys, you, me and the rest of the market wanting to buy OKS. It takes a lot of us little guys to buy what Buffett is selling. Say he's selling 1,000,000 shares at $42.50. First time it gets up there, in total the market (buyers) buy 100,000 shares of that 1 million share offer, then the 2nd, 3rd, 4th time buyers keep buying more but he's still there selling his stock.

Eventually Buffett sells his stock and moves on and if the buyers continue to buy and break the seller then the stock is off to the races. Since we understand chart reading, we can see these patterns forming and we aim to buy **"after"** it breaks-not before! So resistance is $42.50 right?

We (Trading Experts) are buyers when the seller breaks, $42.51 ticks and we're in! In this case, the buyers continued to bid the stock up 10 days in a row! On the 10th day a new seller came in at $47 as you can see it flush up to $47.

Now this time it's different, the last 9 days, the buyers were in control. Look at these big green candlesticks, opening above the prior day's low and trending higher. A sign we love to see, this is probably the Mona Lisa of our swing trades this year because it was a textbook trade.

On the 10th day of this rally, the buyers could not bid the stock up any longer and the sellers took over. Remember we trail our winning trades **versus the prior day's low**.

So let's take a closer look at trailing a winning position **versus the prior day's low**.

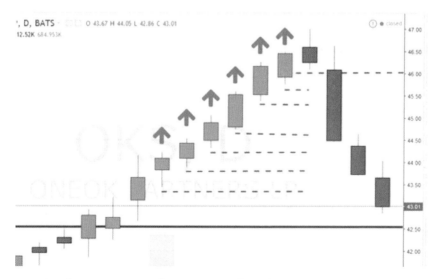

As the swing trade starts to break out and trend higher, we are moving our stop up (red dashed lines) to the prior day's low. We kept doing this as the trade worked in our favor. By Day 3 of the swing, our stop was a profitable stop, so even if it failed we would have made money. With our target being $46+, OKS went as high as $47 and based off our trailing technique we got stopped out at $45.99!

Remember our "Trade of the Week" Game Plan, as you can see below.

Shake P · December 11, 2016

This week our Trade of the Week is OKS. OKS has developed a beautiful macro bull flag pattern, which can also be considered a bullish inverse head and shoulders in some circles. If this takes out highs on some volume, we'd expect a successful breakout.

Trigger: $42.50
Stop: $40.99
Target: $46+

Now did we know $47 would be the top? Not a clue, we just had a game plan and stuck to it. This trade played out perfectly for an 11%+ gain in 10 trading days. Could it be the same seller or a new seller coming in at $47? Maybe, maybe not, we really don't care/ don't know. We just know it's time to leave the table while we're hot. Take our 11% gain and move on. Trading can be simple if you make it simple. We hear all these crazy, elaborate ideas from new traders and it's just too much.

Our idea was as simple as "there's a seller at $42.50, bullish pattern forming, aiming for 5-1 risk reward or better, original stop at $41.99 (risk $.50 per share), trailing vs prior day's low as it works in our favor."

As a result we were able to squeeze $3.50 per share out of this stock for 7-1 risk reward from our original risk. The position was always profitable from our entry! Now we can sit on a beach with a stiff drink under a palm tree while the traders without a plan are sitting through the pain as OKS pulls back to resistance which will/should start to become an area of support.

Game Planning Task

Let's really hammer this idea down, in the group chat post another example where trailing vs the prior day's low would have gotten you out right before the stock reversed a major breakout.

Post your answer in the chat

The Shakeout

We covered the benefits of using stops and we are now going to take a stroll down memory lane on a recent name that shook myself and one of our Alpha Members Valentino out before ripping in our faces. The dirty girl was IT, which was setting up through $126.

As a stock runs to a new high it is usually marked by dumb money chasing the name before the stock reverses and comes back to earth. Now in time as the name eventually gets back to that same high, for IT this would be $126 as there is a psychological wall at that level.

Why, though? It's very simple, everyone who bought $126 months ago is going to look to sell for break even, trust me people do this all the time, even, we do from time to time which you will learn later in *The Round Trip* Lesson.

This is why we avoid looking to buy on the 2nd major retest, as most people are net sellers that second time. The 3rd, 4th, 5th time at major levels, more and more of these sellers are leaving the party, setting the stock ripe for a rip. We tried it the 3rd time however the sellers were still there. IT ticked $126 and went a whopping $.22, no thank you, I will take my paper cut. We took the small loss of less than half a percent and moved on. No harm no fail, maybe I was dumb money buying there, who knows?

published on TradingView.com, January 20, 2018 19:43 UTC
BATSST, D 137.35 ▲ +1.35 (+2.5%) O:134.80 H:138.26 L:134.10 C:137.35
GARTNER INC, D, BATS
vol (10)

Retest Of Support   *Second Retest*

Shake Out

Now IT gets smoked the next day, remember how when a name gets super tight near a level it shows indecision and is usually eventually followed by a bigger move in either direction with Mr Market deciding the stock's fate.

This time the decision was lower for a $10 pull back that we were no part of. After the dust settled, IT started to base near support of $116. The more times a name gets near resistance we want to buy, however the more times a name gets near support the more likely it is to smoke that level lower (what we want to avoid).

Hence why we avoid buying a name that is near support after the 3rd or 4th attempt, usually the exact time most new traders want to buy it because they can get the exact price they want, a bad, bad sign!

After IT holds $116, we buy on the way **up** vs support, Valentino and myself (Ben) buy IT up through $118 with a stop below $116 about $2 risk. It starts to work, however this is the dirty part, the shake out, we were just a few days too early, and it stopped us out as it flushed $116. Our confidence in the name was at an all time low. This is the mental part of trading that makes it more difficult than looking at it now. Now it's super easy "I would have bought back $118 and held it until now" most would boost however we didn't and that's all that matters.

Face harsh realities, worry about achieving your goals, understand how to manage pain to produce progress, and hold yourself accountable.

We took a small paper cut, then got shaken out, and the worst mistake was we didn't get back in (3rd time's a charm). This was a 20% trade we let slip through our fingers by getting shaken out. Keep your risk small and be aware that you might get shaken out a few times before you catch the real ticket!

Game Planning Task

Now we are going to make this a little bit harder. Post an example in the Group Chat, your goal is to find a shake out move. Where if you used a stop at the prior day's low you would have got stopped out, yet the stock came right back and ripped higher. This is a hard one but one that you will see when you start trading.

Post your answer in the chat

Eye on the Percentages

When starting out as a new trader, most are starry eyed at the thought of huge profits from their trading. Focusing on the P&L tends to be a game that is better spent elsewhere. Remember, the stock and Mr Market do not care how much you are up or down in a position, the only person who cares is yourself.

When you have $1,000 in your account making $10,000 seems impossible, or if you have $100,000 in your account making $1,000,000 might also seem just as daunting. What is more important are the percentages you are taking out of the market day in and day out. There are certain names that might take a week to make 10% and others that might take a year. That is why we focus on the percentages. If you are continuously locking in percentages, the money tends to follow in time.

Novice traders believe large positions = larger profits. A hard truth – trading undersized positions produces greater profits over long pull

Name selection is key, there are trades we put on in slow movers like XOM where if we can squeeze 10% it might be a slam dunk where our risk might be half a percent, while in a high fly $30 biotech, we might be risking $1 or 10% to 30% in a few days. You learn this by getting familiar with your name selection and learning how names trade. You learn this by trading them, we can sit here and tell you that names like BAC don't move compared to the leaders (expensive) bank names in the same space but you won't know this until you actually trade them.

The lighter you are in each trade (less money) will be more beneficial as you start to trade. Most new traders want to bet the house on their first trade, when it's the complete opposite. Let's say you bomb your first trade, let's take a look at what it would take to make back the damage you lost.

Table 1 Loss/Recovery Figures	
Percent Loss of Position	Percent Gain Needed to Get Back to Even
-5%	5.3%
-10%	11.1%
-15%	17.6%
-20%	25.0%
-25%	33.3%
-30%	42.9%
-35%	53.8%
-40%	66.7%
-45%	81.8%
-50%	100.0%
-55%	122.0%
-60%	150.0%
-65%	186.0%
-70%	233.0%
-75%	300.0%
-80%	400.0%
-85%	567.0%
-90%	900.0%

The reason why we focus on swing trades is that the risk we put on in each trade can't even fit on this diagram. Our worst ideas that fail tend to fall in the 5% category unless we get caught in a gap down, while most new traders tend to start on the bottom of this chart, where they are willing to lose 50% to 90% to make a few dollars.

Think of anything you excel at, you more than likely sucked at it day 1, trading is no different. For some reason new traders enter the market as if they are Floyd Mayweather, yet have never put on a pair of gloves before or have even practiced! Remember to focus on the percentages, risk 1, 2, 3% and aim to make 5, 6, 7% and after you make 5%, aim to make 6% in the next trade, so on and so forth. You have to build up to the big winners, hit a few singles and doubles first.

Game Planning Task

Share a trading experience you have had where you took a large loss that seemed impossible to climb out of.

If you have not had any trading experience post something you learned from this lesson that you did not know previously.

Post your answer in the chat

Bull's Eye

So you found your A+ stock setting up, it's in the upper right hand corner of it's daily chart, it has been consolidating for some time now, you know where you want to buy, and you know where to get out if you are wrong.

Now the million dollar question is where do you sell this thing when you're right? You've heard it a million times, hold your winners and cut your losers. However at some point you have to sell your winners, right? Yes you're right, at some point we have to sell our winners. Now usually the longer you hold those winners the better they pan out (until they do not) so let's go over two trades in particular where we sold one too early and held the other too long.

"We are what we repeatedly do. Excellence, then, is not an act, but a habit"

Aristotle

Before we jump into those two trades let's set some strict ground rules. For any trade you put on, the target is at min 5X your risk, keyword MINIMUM, none of this mickey mouse stuff where your target is 2:1 risk reward. If you risk $1 per share, you're aiming to make at least $5, if you're risking $2 you're aiming to make $10. So the most basic target is as follows:

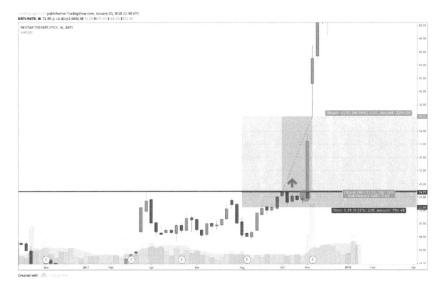

This shows you your risk reward (how to use this tool on tradingview below) which is a good, god I hate to use this word, it's a good *tool* to use. Makes me cringe saying that word, new traders love tools, however this is one that will help keep you focused on the bigger picture. So as we mentioned to start each trade you should always be aiming to make 5 times your risk.

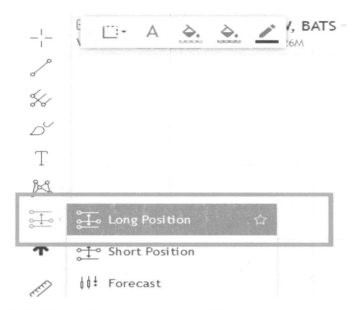

Risk $1 per share aim to make $5+ per share

Risking $100 in the trade aiming to make $500+ per trade

You get the picture. Now there are times when you can't always get 5:1 of course, we are realistic and know that sometimes, you might only be able to squeeze 2, 3 or 4:1 out of a trade, however those are exceptions to the rule. If they are happening more often then you're not following the rules.

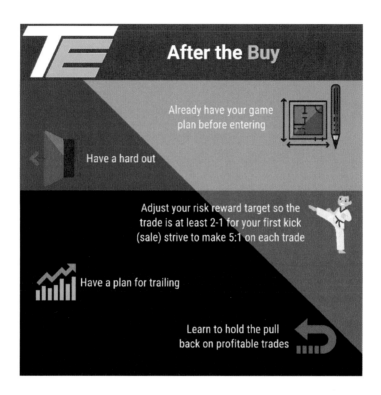

Now let's dive into two trades, to show you the reason why you should have targets and they are written on paper, not set in stone.

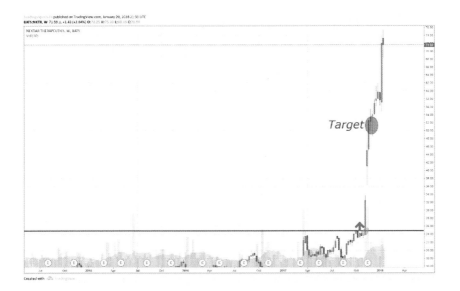

NEXTAR THERAPEUTICS, W, BATS
Vol (10)

Target

Created with

NKTR was a Big Picture Idea that we broke down in the *Risk Elastic* lesson earlier, however for now the topic of discussion is targets. This Big Picture trade had $1 of risk from the $25 entry with the target at $52 which is over 100% higher. The risk reward on this trade was over 27:1 and is currently 300% higher from the entry. Trust me these trades are extremely rare, and you will see how I botched this winner later on. However you can see that prior to this triggering, most (including myself) figured it would have taken a year for this stock to double, yet it only took 9 days and since then is still ripping higher. This is why it's a target. We are aiming for a certain price, however as the stock trades we find out if it is realistic or if we need to be more patient. In this case, holding out longer was the smarter choice. Again with a big fat '*easier said than done*'. I made 65% in this trade and it looks so childish now in hindsight when it's now a 300% winner. More on that later. Now we are going to move onto a swing that I got stuck in for quite some time because it exceeded my target yet I never sold.

ONCE was a swing that we had our eye on all last year and we caught it for an over 40% move from $60 to above $90. I didn't take profits and as we are starting to become more aware, just as fast as they go up, they tend to come down even faster. There are a few key takeaways from this. Huge gap down was on earnings (same reason why we said avoid holding through earnings) and for every winner that you sell too early, it's another trade that was a paper cut that could have turned into a disaster.

I was extremely patient in this ONCE and tied up capital for a much longer period before the mood of this stock turned around in my favor. I eventually sold it a year later for a profit that I could have made the same on the first run up. So remember for your target;

Step 1: Aim for 5X your risk.

Step 2: After the trade starts to show that it's a winner (5%+) you cannot, I repeat, cannot lose money in the trade. (Move Stop to Breakeven)

Step 3: Avoid holding through earnings as long as you can.

Step 4: Rinse and repeat Steps 1-3.

Game Planning Task

Your task here is to post 3 charts in the Group Chat of stocks that have gone far higher in price than you could ever have imagined.

Of those 3 charts try to find bull flags where you could have bought through resistance with a tight stop and caught a decent swing.

Post your answer in the chat

Congrats you already finished 50% of this program! Keep up the hard work! If you're proud of this, say "I'm at the 50% mark!" in the Game Planning Group Chat!

A $60,000 Loss, Who Needs a Game Plan?

There's a reason in trading, that some of the most popular mantras are *"Big wins and small losses,"* and *"Cut your losses and let your winners ride".* It's a simple saying that pretty much notes, *"Live to see another day".* I'll never forget one of my biggest losers that taught me some of the most valuable lessons trading can teach you.

They say you never learn a lesson like when you lose money, and learn I did. This one almost took me out of the business. It was one of the main reasons my partner and I started *Trading Experts.*

Let's take a step back and see just how screwed I was that surmounted a loss equal to a Porsche 911. It's the summer of

2011 and the hot topic of the time was the Debt Ceiling Crisis. If you're not familiar, I'll very briefly summarize; the general public thought the world was going to end if the debt ceiling was not raised. In reality, it's been an arbitrary number our Government has no chance of paying off any time soon. They're going to keep printing and spending money regardless.

Knowing this, CNBC was running their infamous *"MARKETS IN TURMOIL!"* fear-mongering special. It was the popular subject on all the news stations. It all came down to a congressional vote which didn't pass. Now leading up to this, I was sure to get out of all my positions to avoid the knee jerk random reaction that was surely to follow in the markets (shout out to Brexit for a more recent example).

Initially, the market got absolutely smoked. The reaction, coupled with the financial crisis in the rearview mirror, was that the world was indeed ending (financially speaking).

During the month of August 2011, the S&P dropped 200 points from 1300 to 1100. Looking back on the chart, just a small blip, but back then it was absolute mayhem. I began listening to all the fear mongers, thinking this is my chance to hit the big one! The S&P is going to *ZERO* and I'm going to ride it all the way down!

Being inexperienced, I followed into the fear monger's trap and began to short every bounce. I had absolutely no plan, just that I *had* to be right.

At this point I felt invincible, I was able to lock in profits and get flat prior to the market taking a 200 point nosedive, a 15% drop in about two weeks. It can take the overall market 18 months to gain 15%, the same drop took less than 20 trading days. Remember the market is the general public, no one panics during a practice fire drill, but when it's the real thing, everyone goes nuts.

Back to the trades, so I avoid the pain of losing 15% and want to start shorting. Being a trader I want the best bang for my buck, so I find leverage 3X short ETFs. Not only that, I aim for the weakest sectors, so naturally I gravitated to the big banks since they're to blame for the housing bubble. I figure why not short the most hated sector with 3x leveraged ETFs. Now I'll make 30% when this sector pulls in 10%. No brainer right?

The first time around I built into a 500 share short position and cover as the market pulled in resulting in a $2,000 gain in 3 days. A breeze.

Mind you, this was much earlier in my career, when I was a much more brash young man. Over time, the market has a funny way of humbling you. You don't spike the ball as much on your big winners because you know that may lead to forming bad habits such as the carelessness of how you allocate your capital (aka dumb losses). Before I learned these lessons, I thought I was the big-swinging-dick who couldn't be wrong. *"That was the easiest $2000 bucks anyone's made in history!"* I'd exclaim. I'd see some older traders roll their eyes and I would chalk it up to them being jealous. Later I would look back and wish I had taken their dirty looks as a sign that I was being too cocky.

Next time the market bounces, I double my position. Doubling down. Additionally, I begin shorting the S&P. Again, with the 3x leveraged etf. A few days later and the market again flushed. I closed out $6,000 in gains.

KEEP IT GOING! In a week of this market volatility I've locked in more profits than my entire first year of profitable trading. Now I'm feeling like the absolute man. *"It's too easy!"* I gloat.

There was a very wise, experienced trader on the floor at the time, Wilson. He mostly kept to himself but was always observing, as if he were assessing everyone's behavior at all times, gathering information. He was in his 60's and a textbook silver fox. He had been in the markets for upwards of 40 years. He had traded more days than I'd been alive. He was an absolute legend on the floor. When he speaks, which is very rarely, you listen.

As I passed Wilson's desk toward the end of the day, shit-eating grin from ear to ear on my face, I heard him say, *"Young man,"* and I looked over.

He was talking to me. "Young man, you're going too fast. You're going to learn the hard way that it's not that easy."

I told him, "I appreciate the advice but I'm confident about this one." brushing him off.

Now it's time to load the boat, third time's a charm. This time, I have the most conviction it's going to work, I start telling my friends about this home run trade that I will retire from. So now I short across the board:

1000 shares 3x leveraged Banks short (FAZ)

1000 shares 3x leveraged S&P short (SPXU)

1000 shares 3x leveraged NASDAQ short (SQQQ)

1000 shares 3x leveraged Russell 2000 short (TZA)

My plan is as simple as short into resistance, cover into support and lock in profits. The problem was that I didn't plan for things to go wrong; no stop loss, no out. In my head, as with most newbies, it is the idea that for **every** point the SPY falls, I'll net $4,000. I was completely focused on the end goal, without putting any thought into all the different possible outcomes.

Now this 3rd time is going to be the BIG one, I'm not going to cover when the SPY falls back down from 130 to 110. I'm going to hold onto my whole position because *this time* it's going to 90. $100,000 plus profit and then a long vacation.

At this time, Wilson's words of wisdom began to ring in my head a bit. *"It's not that easy."* He was talking about the grind of trading. There are no overnight successes. It's a skill just like any other job, and to be great, it takes repetition along with constant learning and improving. Being young and naive, again, I brush it off.

I have these 4 positions on 1,000 shares each, and the market starts to slightly pull in each day, in my favor. However, it's not a panic-like breakdown, more of a slow, methodical fall, but not as much as the previous two times. The SPY was at 131 the day I got short; day 2 126; day 3 119. I still have some green on the screen, except it's much smaller than usual. (Now, I would consider the possibility of buyers starting to come in.)

Day 4, the market gaps up above 130 and is off to the races! The game just severely changed! Now I'm starting to get hurt, I couldn't even describe the pit in my stomach. But you know what, I already locked in $8,000, I'll let it ride against me, I *know* I'm right!

The market decides to rally 100 points in my face and I start to add to my losing position around 1400, which is the first time I learned how dumb it is to add to a loser. The market starts to stall around 1400 and pull back into 1300. Now I really feel like a big dog. Faced with a big loss, I added to the trade and imposed my will upon the market. TERRIBLE lesson.

Except there is a peculiar thing about the market. It always has a funny way of humbling you when you feel invincible. You can't always be right even if you think that's the case. I was so focused on being *the man* I had not thought about the basics like support and resistance. The entire trade I was shorting at resistance and taking profit into support, great trading, **when you have a plan.**

Generally, when a stock breaks through resistance, it will retest this level and have it become support. The market gives me one last chance to save face and not get my face ripped off. It pulled in to 1300 (previous resistance that has now turned into support), but I am so oblivious to this fact, I'm still dreaming of my $100,000 payday. Was I going to get out of this trade to break even? I've been through too much pain for that! I was worried I'd look stupid, and you know what happened? The market made me look stupid.

The rally of all rallies proceeded this gap down. The S&P blew through 1400, 1500, 1600 and my dreams of a $100k pay day had very quickly developed into a crippling loss. I was sick to my stomach when I finally had to cut my loss. I rotted in the position, trying to talk myself into being right, finding every bearish article I could and reading it as gospel. I had no stop-loss and no real plan in the case I was wrong, and oh, was I wrong.

There were so many indicators in this trade telling me I was wrong but I was too stubborn to pay attention to them. They say the best lessons are always learned from losing money, and this is the trade I'll never forget. If only I had listened to my mentor, I would have saved a lot of money.

"The market can stay irrational longer than you can stay solvent."

John Maynard Keynes

Now, whenever I feel myself getting too excited about a trade that's going my way, I think about Wilson's advice. To be a successful trader, you have to be as emotionless as possible. You can't marry a trade, you'll never end up on the right side of it. This game takes patience coupled with the utmost discipline. There are no overnight successes, it's hard work every single day at improving your skill set. This can't be stressed enough. Though I lost a lot of money in this devastating loss, it's taught me life long lessons, and that's priceless. I never traded the same after this humbling experience. I wasn't the stereotypical abrasive Wall Street trader. I made sure to become much more calculated and risk-averse. It's about longevity in this business.

Since this trade, I've had thousands fail, except the difference is that as a professional trader we focus on big wins and small losses. You have to be able to admit when you're wrong, or else your tenure in this business will be a short one. The new trader loses big and cuts his winner's too quickly until he is properly trained. Even when properly trained, you need to constantly adapt your skillset and review every trade as you never stop learning. Trading is all about evolving and constantly learning while adjusting game plans on the regular. If you ever meet a trader who says he's done learning or knows everything, he's full of it.

10 Fatal Flaws

FATAL FLAW

H ere are 10 fatal errors made by misguided traders who are destined to fund the accounts of more skilled traders.

1. A trader must have a trading plan with well-defined entries, exits, and position size before they make any trades. Trading with no plan creates random results, and the profits that are won as a result of chance will eventually return to their rightful owners.

2. Traders must have an edge to be profitable. The traders that have discipline, have done their homework about historical price action, and stay in control of their emotions will make money.

3. The biggest mistake that the majority of traders make at all levels, is that they trade too big. Big position sizes cause emotions to run high, infringing on reason. Big losses are also more financially and emotionally

devastating. The position size of a trade should never put a trader's lifestyle or trading career at risk.

4. When the markets open, the trader must have the discipline to follow the plan they created when the market was closed. No system will work if the trader does not have the discipline to follow it.

5. When a trader's desire to be right is greater than the desire to make money, they will illogically let a losing trade run to avoid admitting that they are wrong.

6. Fear of giving back a small profit will cause a trader to miss a bigger winning trade. Most profitability is based on the big winning trades. A winning trade should not be exited until there is a good reason to do so.

7. If a trader does not take their original stop loss, they will allow small losses to become big losses. Big losses generally are what cause a trader to be unprofitable. Many good trading systems become profitable simply by removing the big losses from the trading results.

8. Traders that do not account for events outside the known bell curve can be ruined. Events that have never happened before can happen. Stop losses and position sizing are the insurance policies against the sudden risk of ruin.

9. Traders with too much hubris will eventually make a decision that insures a fatal trading result.

10. Personal predictions have no value, because the future does not exist in the present moment, no matter how strong a trader's convictions.

Game Planning Task

Share a fatal flaw that you might have fallen victim to prior to joining Trading Experts, or a flaw that you are working on improving and how you plan to rid that flaw from your trading.

Post your answer in the chat

You are officially at the 60% mark! Only 40% to go! Drop "I'm at the halfway point and I learned ...." in the Game Planning Group Chat!

Shoulda Let Em Steal It

(Where the failed carjacking took place)

I t's a fall Friday evening in northern New Jersey, my friend *Big Papi* calls me and before I can say hello he fires off:

"We're going out tonight. Leave wifey at home, 1 OAK tonight!"

He goes on to explain that the whole crew (Wrench, Gross Rev, Shake and a few others) are coming and the pre game's starting at Wrench's loft on the Upper East side. I know Gross Rev will be there, ready to tell me about all the money he made last week.

Wrench will be there in a full 3 piece suit, even though no one wears ties in clubs unless you're a bouncer or promoter who takes his job way too seriously.

Side note -- once Wrench came out of the bathroom stall at the office wearing his vest and jacket, he went to the bathroom fully suited up with a vest on, who does that?

Wrench was maybe 5'4" and 130 pounds soaking wet, so he would not be mistaken for security, nor was he the most outgoing, so no one would mistake him for either a bounce or promoter. Shake (my future business partner) was going to be there as well with a few other traders from the desk. The night was setting up to be what my college buddies would refer to as "*a movie*".

His loft was about a 30 min drive, however with 500+ horsepower under the hood, I could get there in half the time. I see a liquor store sign up ahead off to the side of the highway and I slow down to grab the usual 12 pack of Corona for the pre game. Lord knows I'm going to have to blow a stupid amount of money on overpriced Grey Goose at the club later might as well hit a cheap bit when the opportunity presents itself.

I live in a very safe town, voted one of the top 20 safest towns in NJ, as a result I always leave my car running whenever I'm running a quick errand. Being a creature of habit, I left the Aston Martin top down, music bumping & engine running in front of the liquor store. News to me, the town I was passing through was *NOT* listed on top 20 safest towns. While I'm checking out, and having an idle conversation with the cashier, all of a sudden we hear my engine revving as I'm at the counter paying.

The cashier looks at me, *"Is that your car out front?"*

I reply nonchalantly *"Oh, it's probably one of my friends passing by, messing with me or something."*

Yes I realize how insane/stupid my thinking was. I was by myself. What random friend would be passing by on a busy highway, hop out their car and rev my engine as a joke? Boy was I naive at that moment (hence the 2.4 GPA license plate).

As I walk out of the liquor store, with my hands in the air, as if to say *"Yo what's up!"* to Wrench or Shake, or whoever this imaginary friend may be. Waiting to hear my buddies respond, I kept walking. To my surprise, it certainly wasn't any of my friends messing with me.

I walk out to a man wearing a ski mask trying to swiftly take off with my Aston. Just then the getaway car pulls up, a blacked out Infiniti G35 Sedan with 3 other ski masked individuals screeching to a halt. The guys in the Sedan start yelling at the robber in my car, ***"WHAT THE FUCK IS TAKING YOU SO LONG?!"***

At that moment, I wasn't thinking, *"Let them steal it, then I'll clear $200,000 from my insurance policy"*. Not even close. It was purely fight or flight mode, and these losers were NOT stealing my Aston.

All of this happened in mere seconds, my 12 pack drops from my hand and shatters as I dive over the passenger seat and pull the keys from the ignition. As I try to grab the carjacker, he stands up on the seat and dives head first into the rear passenger window of the getaway car and they peel out back onto the highway with his legs dangling out the window.

They drifted back onto the highway and disappeared into the night. The cashier comes running out, and loses his shit, as I find it quite funny. He's throwing his hands up in the air yelling, *"Holy shit man, they tried to steal your Aston Martin?!*

Damn man, I'll call the police. Why would you leave this car running?!"

I walk over to pick up the 12 pack and come to realize they are all broken except two :(

(RIP to the 12 pack in the blue bag, 10/12 broken during the failed carjacking.)

As this guy is losing his mind about my car, I'm just thinking '*ah damn my Coronas are done'.* I couldn't even get the Stopped-A-Robbery discount and had to pay retail for my second 12 pack of the night. As amazed as the cashier was, it was back to business when I asked for it on the house. I just received a simple shoulder shrug of an employee with no power.

I found out weeks later that same night, a half mile down the road, 4 Mercedes Benz were stolen -- so clearly these were low level car jackers. They could steal 4 cars out of a parking lot, but the engine running in a convertible Aston Martin, no dice.

Eventually I'll come up with a funny joke like, *"How many carjackers does it take to steal a running Aston Martin?"* Lesson learned on their part (click the paddle shifter before redlining the car in neutral) and they could have made a clean getaway.

For me, the main lesson was that if I didn't take action I would have banked it that night, but stopping them was worth every penny. I still leave my car running just for the hell of it. I asked the store owner for a copy of the tape as it would be the funniest to watch it unfold. However I needed to file a police report, team no snitching.

After I buy the second 12 pack of the evening, I finally arrive at Wrench's as he's deciding which suit he should wear, a grey plaid 3 piece or a double breasted navy pinstripe. I start laughing and explain my ride over; of course he isn't even the slightest bit impressed or interested. The kind of person that needs to one-up everything and always tries extra hard to play it cool.

When the rest of the group arrived, most couldn't believe it and were shocked. I bet Gross Rev secretly hoped it did get stolen! As for the night, let's just say it peaked with the near car-jacking. 1Oak was 1Oak -- loud music, hot girls who only care about your wallet, and $15 bottles of Fiji water.

Game Planning Task

Share a story where you had to make a split second fight or flight decision.

Share your story in the chat

Keep up the consistency, only 25% left to go! Let's hear it in the chat "I only have 25% left to finish Game Planning, I will complete it by (insert your deadline)

9 Secrets

If you do not know who Jesse Livermore is, he is one of the most legendary traders who has ever lived. Below are 9 trading secrets that he lived and died by, so let's take a moment to learn from one of the greats!

1. "Money is made by **sitting**, not trading."

2. "It takes **time** to make money."

3. "It was never my thinking that made the big money for me, it always was **sitting**."

4. "Nobody can catch **all** the fluctuations."

5. "The desire for constant action irrespective of underlying conditions is responsible for many losses in Wall Street even among the professionals, who feel that they must take home some money every day, as though they were working for regular wages."

6. "Buy right, sit tight."

7. "Men who can both be right and sit tight are uncommon."

8. "Don't give me timing, give me time."

9. "There is a time for all things, but I didn't know it. And that is precisely what beats so many men in Wall Street who are very far from being in the main sucker class. There is the plain fool, who does the wrong thing at all times everywhere, but there is the Wall Street fool, who thinks he must trade all the time. Not many can always have adequate reasons for buying and selling stocks

daily – or sufficient knowledge to make his play an intelligent play."

Game Planning Task

Share which secret caught you most by surprise.

Share your answer in the chat

Where's This Thing Going To Open?

"**W**here's this thing going to open?! Down $5 bucks, down $10?!" I panicked. It was late April in 2015, I was coming off my first $10k week, I felt like Jesse Livermore. I began swinging heavier positions in riskier names because I was getting addicted to feeling like the top dog on the desk. There are a lot of egos on a trading floor, arguably more-so than in any other business. On our desk in particular, we had a whole slew of BSDs like Jack, Mr. X, Wrench and my personal mentor, whom we'll call *Beast* because he is a *beast*. After years of lessons and going through the constant roller coaster of emotions, I've learned that cockiness and arrogance just aren't worth it. You will never read in a book about the pit you'll feel in your stomach when a loss is too great. Ask the top fund managers around, the biggest aspect of being a successful trader is risk management.

I was finally earning respect on the floor after putting up a 10-bagger (aka $10k week). Word spread quickly on the floor and even Wilson was impressed with how quickly I was improving. However, the $10k week wasn't enough. Greed is kicking in and I have my sights set on a $40k month. I wanted to squeeze out *more*.

Heading into a weekend, it's wise for an active trader to take some risk off the table if you're swinging heavy positions. So much unexpected news can come out over the weekend, you don't want to catch yourself on the wrong side of it Monday morning. Let me tell you about when I did and quickly went from top-dog to dog-shit.

I killed it that week, felt like everything I bought would rip. I was in the zone, everything was starting to click. Going into the weekend, I had a very tough decision to make. I was holding 400 shares of Amazon from $382 with $380 being my stop, risking about $800:

$382 entry price - $380 stop = $2 risk

$2 risk X 400 shares = $800 risk

This was a couple months after Amazon started toying with the public that it wanted to have drones deliver packages within hours of ordering, so Amazon was a hot stock.

This news coupled with the bull flag sounded like a homerun in the making. The top of the bull flag was $388 so my thinking was that if I could hold on and catch the breakout, Amazon could be north of $400. If I held my 400 shares for an $18 gain, I'd be looking at a $7200 gain on $800 risk, a 9:1 risk/reward!

BUT, my rule has always been, clean it up before the weekend. The name of the game is risk management. Cut down all of your positions, you don't want that much overnight risk. I was on such a hot-streak though, how could I not let it ride? I'm currently up just over $2000 on the trade so

I'm already at a favorable risk-reward, why not take some risk off the table? Why not book some profit and make it a risk-free trade? Because I was too focused on the payday, selling it at $400+ and not thinking about risk management.

(The circled candle is how the AMZN daily candle closed that Friday)

I remember that weekend as one of the better weekends I've had. I was crushing it trading, just had a big pay day, and was gaining more and more respect from my colleagues. My mentor Beast was finally taking my trade ideas more seriously. When you have a mentor in trading, they're like a father you're always trying to impress. For most of my career leading up to this, my ideas for the most part had been brushed off and not taken as seriously as some of the more senior traders. But it was all changing, and I was on top of the world. I slacked off that weekend and didn't put in my usual detailed chart work on Sunday as I knew I already had Amazon waiting to explode $10+ on Monday, so I didn't have that killer instinct. It's about to be an easy week ahead, another week of counting cash.

I wake up Monday morning, check my phone, and I see a MarketWatch notification I'll never forget:

BREAKING: FAA SHUTS DOWN AMAZON'S HOPES OF DRONE DELIVERY

Holy Hell. Out of NOWHERE, they drop this news. Earlier, Amazon had written a letter to the FAA saying their strict laws regarding commercial use of drones are standing in the way of innovation.

The Federal Aviation Administration (FAA) came out with a huge press release Sunday night saying they did not intend to change their stance on drones in any shape or form.

This should send Amazon stock into a frenzy as the rumor of their drone delivery had been propping up the stock the entire quarter. My overjoyed weekend turned into a hellish Monday fast. I check my phone to see where the bids are in premarket trading, down $5. There goes my $2k gain in a split second. Great.

By the time I got into the office, news had spread that I was very long Amazon. Traders generally know their colleague's trading-size, so when people heard I had $160,000 of Amazon stock over the weekend with this negative news out, everyone had something to say.

Wrench, the snotty, entitled guy who walked around with daddy's money snickered, *"Trading a little too big for your britches, huh?"* I told him to kept it moving.

Jack, the old-school, stereotypical office enforcer was slapping his mini baseball bat as usual, *"It's not all rainbows and butterflies is it?!"* Thanks for the help, chief.

Beast, my mentor, sat me down and offered some advice, *"In this business, sometimes you're on top and sometimes you're not. But, you can't put yourself in a position to get hurt. In a downturn, you've seen it, 50% of the office disappears as these beta-traders* with no discipline get wiped out. I agree that when you're hot you push it a bit, but you know the dangers of holding onto that much stock over a weekend, in Amazon no* *less!"* I told him I appreciated the wise words and I wouldn't forget that lesson.

(*Beta-traders are known as traders who kill it when the times are great, by getting long any setup in a high-beta name and having success. During choppy times or bear markets, beta-traders are generally the first to be wiped out, losing all their trading capital, aka blowing up their account.)

It's around 9:15 now and pre-market trading becomes more active. When a position gaps against you, you never want to get out in the pre-market. Pre-market trading is characterized by light volumes and huge spreads. If you get out of a trade because it gaps down on you pre-market, then it rips off the open, you're going feel like a jackass because it was just a few orders that caused you to sell. So I walked in and it's now down $5.50 with bids at $379.50 and offers at $383 (remember, my original sell-stop was $380 and I walked in Monday to a price below that).

(The difference in the bid-ask spread in this high priced, high-beta stock on 400 shares was $1200. In a stock like Bank of America, BAC, a low-beta and relatively low-priced stock the spread might be $.01. So on 400 shares, the difference is only $4.)

You can see why it's not ideal getting out premarket with such a costly spread.

All of a sudden, a seller came in just slapping down bids, and the price began to drop faster than a penny off the top of the Empire State Building. *"Where's this fucking thing going to open?! Down $5 bucks? 10?!"* The general rule of thumb when swinging a position and it gaps against you, is to wait for the first 15-minute candle to close and put your stop at the low of that candle, in hopes of salvaging the trade.

Amazon opens immediately down $8 and I can't take the pain and just immediately puke half my position at $378, for a loss of $800. I was not following any sort of rules other than letting fear take control of my trading.

Remember, my original stop was $380 but it opened up below, so I never had a chance of getting out there. I lost $800 on those 200 shares alone, when my game plan was to risk that on the entire position of 400 shares. I'm going to treat these 200 shares right, wait for the 15-minute candle to close and maybe I'll get lucky. (*You never want to be hoping you get lucky, more often than not it ends up going very badly.)

The 15-minute candle makes a low at $376.50 so I put my stop below that figure. It gives me a glimmer of hope as it rallies the next 10 minutes, only to shatter my dreams and flush through $376.50 leaving me with a substantially greater than expected loss. On a position I went into the weekend +$2000, I finished Monday -$3000, a quick $5000 swing. I had given up 50% of my profits from my best week in just one day.

Looking back, if I had more experience, I would have sold half my position (200 shares) that Friday. I would have booked $1000 and more than covered my risk in the trade. Monday still wouldn't have been fun but I would have protected my profits and had a break even trade instead of losing $3,000. Then again, if I had done that, I wouldn't have been able to tell you this story!

(The arrow candle is that following Monday's daily candle)

They say you never learn a lesson like losing money. Believe me, this one will stick with me for a while. It was more than the money lost that Monday, it was about how quickly my hard work and smart executions from the week prior were wiped out. If you trade like a loose cannon, that's going to happen more and more until it takes you out for good.

I always think back to Beast's words noting the importance of risk-management. You often hear, the most important part of your job on Wall Street is to keep your job. Starting to trade is easy, but surviving day-in and day-out maintaining the utmost discipline is the hard part. Being cocky can be your greatest downfall and having an ego will only help you to lose money.

> *Be smart. Game plan. Have patience. Manage your risk. It's the only way to survive.*

You are almost there, just 10% left and you will be passing the finish line! Let's hear 2 things about your trading that has improved in the Game Planning Chat as you have already completed 90% of it!

The 1 Share Tough Guy

As swing traders, we are given a gift and a curse, the gift is obvious, we are able to exploit charts for short term movements with very little risk, the curse is that we sometimes look too closely and miss the bigger picture.

Looking back over some of my better trades this year (you will do this at the end of the lesson) and we will notice that most ended up higher than where we sold. This was the case more often in the trades where I was able to sell at least 10% higher. Sure at the time, selling on the doji at highs after a solid run and the stock pulled back for a few days making the trade look perfect, then we forget about it.

After this 30% kick and the stock selling off the next day in FTNT, who wouldn't feel like that was a great trade on 1% risk? Then we forget about the name and look back a month later.....

Then we feel like a big stupid idiot, our tough guy 30% chop, now looks like a baby trade when the stock is up 50% and showing no signs of stopping.

I've done this, you've done it, anyone who makes money at trading has done this. I said make money, bc traders who lose money only buy and sell lower or short and cover higher.

Now why is this? Ego or greed, plausible? The real answer is a lack of patience, in a commission free world with impressively cool platforms, it's never been more fun and easier to be impatient.

Would we rather be more profitable or have fun running around in circles, selling winners to go and try to find other winners?

Changing this is easy, we just need to start becoming 1 Share Tough Guy's. Holding 1 share, or an inconsequential dollar amount of stock for you is the goal, your 1 share equivalent is going to be different than the next, so pick the share or dollar amount and stick to it with the goal of slowly increasing it over time. The goal is after you take your trade with the larger portion of your position, you set a breakeven stop for your tough guy position.

By setting the bar so low, you or I will not care about the 1 share, or the few hundred dollars in the name. The same as how easily you were able to start saving $5 a week and now you are most likely saving 50X that. If you are not saving weekly at this point, please slap yourself.

Now 1 share is boring and that's the point, you won't care giving 1 share back $10 to breakeven, and by not caring, you'll be able to hold those winners much longer. In time after you (and I) consistently see those quick 10% winners turn into slower 50-100% winners, the overall lesson of patience will continue to get hammered into our skulls. We will then continue to be able to size up in these tough guy positions and really see how long it takes to hold a position long term.

So if you want to join me in being a 1 share tough guy, or your equivalent of 1 share, let's see who can get to the first 100% winner first!

Game Planning Task

Go through your top 5 trades in the last 2 years and see where they are trading today!

1. **Post how much they are up from your entry**

2. **Post how much they are up from where you last sold**

3. **If you really want to go the extra mile, post the daily charts showing your entry and exit and where they are now percentage wise from question 1 and 2.**

Post your answers in the chat so we can all learn from them!

Trade Journal

In life, we learn the most from our mistakes, if you think back to when you were a child there were plenty of these. In trading it's no different, the best traders in the world are only right about 40% of the time and they learn the most from those 60% of failed trades. After a trade is closed, we fill out a trade report card, so we can look back and see how we executed our game plan. Was it good/bad/horrible etc, as you look through your trade, you will see where your strengths and weaknesses are.

This is very easy to do, open your Goal Setting Document and open up Step 2 Trading Recap. If you do not have one yet let Ben G know and he will create one for you. Or you can create your own Trade Journal and journal your first trade, an example is below. Now you want to hold off on trading, until you get into Alpha before you start trading, however you can get your journal ready now.

On Tradingview, draw out your chart, circle your entry, circle your stop, where you sold, then click the camera to take a photo of your chart. Insert the chart into your journal and recap your trade!

For this trade, the recap is short and simple.

- Entry 160.05

- Stop day 1 was $156.89 ($3 risk), day 2 was $159.90 (breakeven), then trailing low of day for the next 3 days.

- Sold $169 ($9 per share profit)

Stock ran up into $170 which was a soft resistance level, zooming out, and saw a doji forming at highs, upped the stop to the current low of day and got ticked out, stock eventually started to roll over and will most likely come back to my price or lower.

Initial risk reward was 3 to 1, improvement for next trade like this, buy heavier when the sector is breaking out.

Short and simple, if you're more of a stats guy or gal, use Tradersync.com is an easy to use free site where you can journal your entry and exit, it will show you your hit rate, average profit, loss, etc.

Most of our Alpha traders do both, daily. For every single trade. We would strongly recommend you to pick up these successful trading habits.

Game Planning Task

In the Group Chat post a screenshot of your trade journal book, document or your Tradersync account! Keep these

close by, once you get into Alpha you will be using them daily!

Share your answer in the chat

The Entrepreneur, Manager, and the Technician

Entrepreneur Manager Technician

The Entrepreneur, Manager, and the Technician... Which one are you?

The correct answer is all three of them, it only matters which facet you excel at. The most important part of trading is finding a consistent system that works for you.

The three people inside your mind and inside your trades are either hurting or helping you and that's what we need to determine and improve on.

The Entrepreneur - When looking at trades, can you see where you believe the stock can go, and in time does it go there? Are you realistic with your expectations or is every trade your next million dollar trade? The Entrepreneurial part of your thinking looks at each trade as a business to run, how will this trade make me more profitable, give me the freedom to do more of the things I enjoy, etc. Or are you over enthusiastic and expect the stock you bought at $50 yesterday to be at $100 tomorrow just because you bought it.

Positions				☐ – ☐ ×
Symbol	Position	Price	Marked P&L	+/- Position ▾ Cos
NTES	100	293.44	+4,249.00	+12.35
FB	500	134.08	+1,505.20	+2.21
X	400	41.57	-514.08	-1.2852
CELG	0	118.99	-45.00	0.00
DOX	0	60.06	-32.00	0.00
BIVV	0	47.50	-584.70	0.00
XPO	0	52.64	-223.00	0.00
MBLY	0	47.46	-343.89	0.00
All	1,000		+4,011.54	+1.83

The main factors of your Entrepreneurial Mindset focus on:

- ☼ How the overall trade went

- ☼ What you did well

- ☼ What needs improvement

- ☼ How will you implement these improvements in the next trade

The Manager - When you put on the trade are you able to buy it at the price you set in your game plan? The Technician inside of you found the proper entry price. Was the Manager inside you able to buy when you said you would?

After the trade is placed, the Manager inside you makes sure to keep the plan the same, the stop the same and the profit targets the same. If you are able to stick to your original game plan from your Technician side that is usually the best outcome, but as you start to trade the greed and fear tend to come out. If you are able to stick to the stops and profit targets you should be successful in the long run.

The main factors of your Manager side focus on:

- ⚡ Were your entries, stops, and profit targets in your game plan stuck to?
- ⚡ Did you get out too early or too late? (Fear)
- ⚡ Did you hold on or give back too much profit? (Greed)

The Technician - How you look at charts and identify a good trade idea vs a bad trade idea. How you formulate the game plan for the trade, how you determine your ideal risk reward. Ideally you want to aim for 5 to 1 or more on your trades and 10 to 1 on our A+ trades that we will go over later on.

The main factors of the Technician aspect focus on:

- ⚡ Chart work
- ⚡ Using layers of probability to determine the effectiveness of each set up (moving averages, sector,

your time frame, relative strength/weakness, results of earnings, etc.)

- ☀ Identifying Strong stocks to buy (stocks in the top right corner of the chart)
- ☀ Identifying Weak stocks to short (stocks in the bottom right corner of the chart)
- ☀ Game plan prior to the entry

You will see over time that one of these three will stick out the most, the one that is helping you and also the one that is hurting you. Are you having trouble increasing your position size, or are your gains and losses on trades reckless?

As you go through your trades and game plans you will be able to find your strengths and weaknesses over time, and when you can recognize these problem areas you can improve them.

Your entrepreneurial mindset keeps you engaged and forever making improvements, your manager mindset gives it order, and the technician in you puts you to work. You need all three working in tandem or your business will eventually end and this is one tough business to be in!

Game Planning Task

Take a moment and think of all you have learned so far and reflect on some of the major lessons you have learned and let's hear them in the chat!

Share your answer in the chat

Congratulations on Completing the Game Planning Program!

See that wasn't so hard! If you follow the lessons such as proper risk reward, correct trailing techniques and finding the proper stocks to buy then you will be ahead of 90% of the market (since most traders do not take the time to formulate proper game plans).

You can smile knowing that you officially reached the end of this program and you did an amazing job! Before we **summarize** the main takeaways from our *Game Planning Program*, we have a request and it would be greatly appreciated if you would comply.

If you found the information that we presented has made you better understand trading and investing, then all we ask is that you leave us a nice review on our Facebook page!

Summary

1. Price Matters
2. Always use a stop
3. Risk reward of 5:1 Min
4. Have a game plan prior to entry
5. Stick to that game plan
6. Learn from your mistakes
7. Review your trades
8. Lock in profits

Congrats on completing the Game Planning Program! To move up to Chart Reading, one last thing to do!

Game Planning Certified Test

Why do we aim for 5-1 risk reward or better in our trade setups?

Post In Chat

Why do we cut our losers fast and let our winners ride as long as possible?

Post In Chat

Describe your A+ setup. Be sure to detail what you can utilize as a layer of probability on your side (Eg: strong earnings on a strong chart looking to get long a bull flag). The more detail the better.

Post In Chat

Formulate a complete game plan of your A+ setup. Please include the chart, the pattern drawn out, your entry, stop, target, relationship to it's moving averages, when it reports earnings and any other information you feel is important.

Post In Chat

If you are buying a breakout, how will your game plan differ if the stock closes *above* the resistance level vs at the low of day?

Post In Chat

Which lesson helped you the most/changed your mindset regarding trading and why?

Post In Chat

Which lesson confused you the most that we can work on improving?

Post In Chat

A _____ order is an order that buys or sells the stock immediately at the best available price. These orders do NOT guarantee a price, but they DO guarantee immediate execution.

a) Limit
b) Stop
c) Market
d) All or None

Post In Chat

What is your favorite chart pattern to execute and why? Be as specific as possible.

Post In Chat

A strong stock with great earnings has built a nice base. You enter long when it breaks resistance and the stock finishes up big, on high volume. How should you treat your position?

a) Sell it all, take the cash!

b) Reduce some stock to pay for the trade, and hold the majority of the position.

c) Don't sell a single share, it's going to the moon!

d) Go out and buy a lambo -- you've got it all figured out.

Amazon is trading around all time highs, all everyone has been talking about is how much sales they've done in the past few months with brick & mortar stores like Walmart & Target getting crushed in the process. They have earnings after the close today -- what do you do?

a) Buy the stock -- easy 100 points!

b) Go short the stock -- the retail traders are usually wrong

c) Don't touch the stock -- earnings are ALWAYS a gamble

Final Question ---- what is the name of the game?!

a) Big money baby!
b) Risk management
c) Buy low and sell high
d) Buy high and sell low

Made in the USA
Monee, IL
13 October 2022

aa09f79a-8c16-44f9-8d3b-4071cf03425fR01